Contents

Some words are printed in bold, **like this**. You can find out what they mean by looking in the glossary.

What is death?

Death is the ending of life. When people die, their bodies stop working. The heart stops beating and the brain stops functioning.

People have always wanted to learn the secret of living forever. In ancient times, explorers and scientists searched for the secret of eternal life. The truth is, nothing can live forever. Everyone and everything will die in time. Plants, animals, and people all die. Death is a natural part of life.

All living things eventually die, including plants, animals, and people.

Scary feelings

Even though death is a normal part of life, it is often difficult to deal with. If a person knows he or she is going to die, they can feel scared, lonely, and sad. The person usually does not want life to end. They wonder what will happen to loved ones who are left behind.

When a family member or a friend dies, the people who are left behind feel upset and scared too. They miss the person who has died and wonder what life will be like without him or her.

Death is difficult to deal with at any age.

Case study

Paul was 12 when his father died in a car accident. When his mum told him, Paul felt like someone had punched him in the chest. He screamed and pushed his mother away. Paul was angry at his father, even though he knew the accident wasn't his father's fault. He was also upset by all the friends and relatives who came to visit during the first few days after the death. Paul just wanted to be left alone.

Causes of death

Death can be caused by a number of factors.

Natural causes

Natural causes are the most common reason a person dies. Natural causes mean that a person dies of old age. As a person ages, his or her body does not work as well as it did before. Cells, organs, and body systems break down. As these parts of the body wear out or become damaged, the person can become ill and die.

Diseases

Some **diseases** can last a long time. Cancer, heart disease, and lung disease are serious illnesses. Although many people survive these diseases, others will die from them. It usually takes months or years before these diseases become **fatal**.

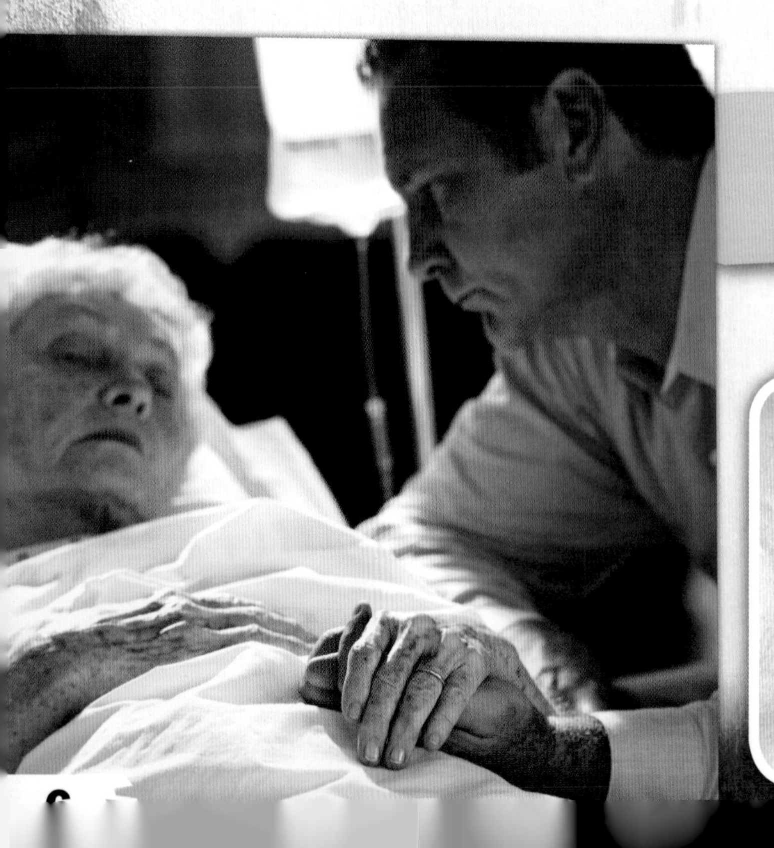

Most people die after living long, full lives.

NEWSFLASH

In the United Kingdom in 2005, the leading causes of death were:

1. Heart disease
2. Stroke
3. Cancer

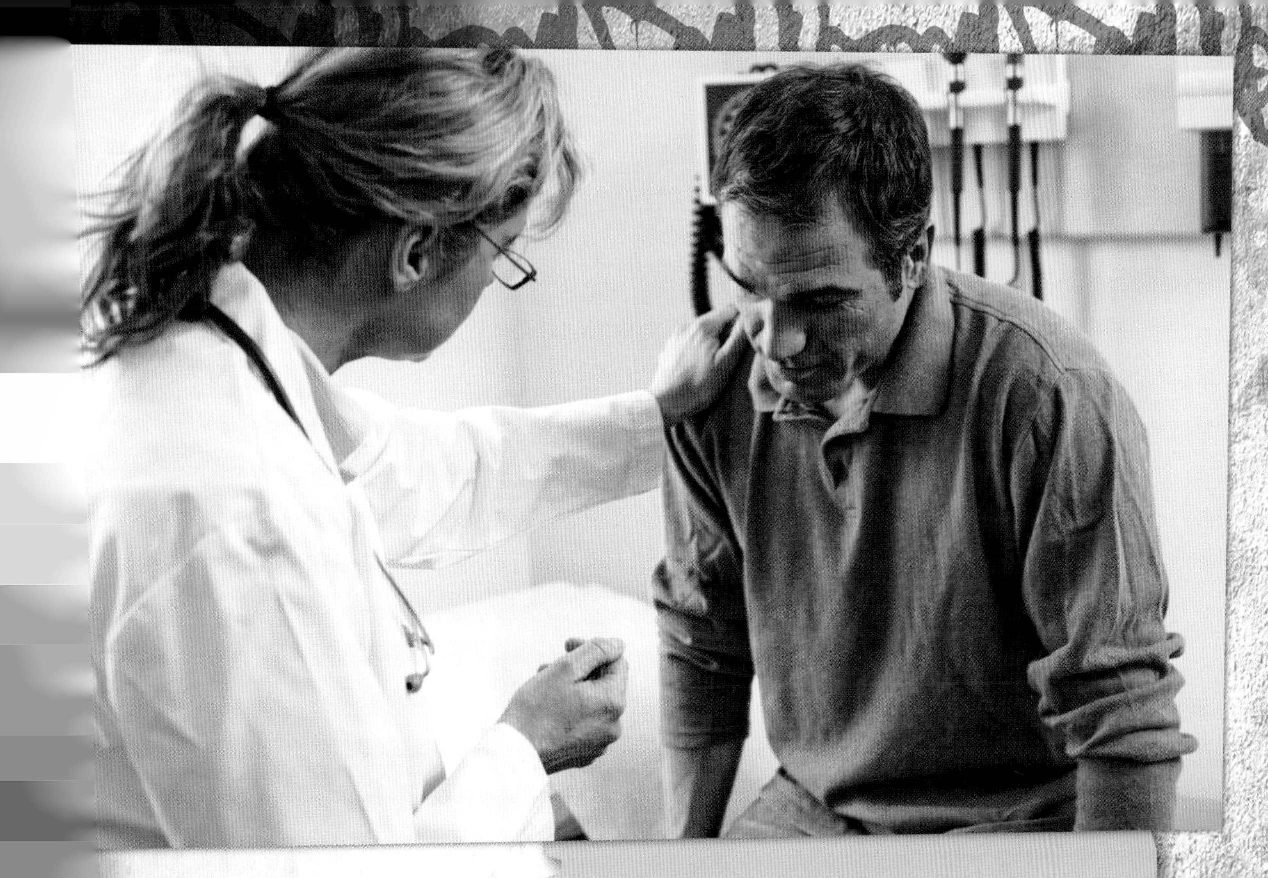

Sometimes death occurs after a sudden illness.

Other people die after a short illness. They might get a very bad infection or another medical condition that hurts the body so badly that it can no longer function. Some people are born with serious illnesses and may die at a younger age because of these conditions.

Will I die from this?

Everyone gets sick at one time or another. Very few people die from common illnesses. You shouldn't worry that you are going to die just because you don't feel well.

NEWSFLASH

Pets can also die from natural causes. People are often very close to their pets and feel like they are members of the family. However, when a pet dies, its family's feelings are not usually taken seriously. People might say, "It was just a dog" or "You can always get another cat." People who say things like this usually mean well, but their comments do not help.

Car accidents are a leading cause of accidental death.

More causes

Natural causes and diseases are not the only things that can cause death. Death can also be caused by an accident or some kind of **violence**. These types of death are not called natural causes, because they do not happen because of natural events.

Accidental deaths

Accidents are a very common cause of death. They are the leading cause of death for people under 45 years old, including children and teenagers. There are many different types of accidents. Some accidents happen when people are travelling from one place to another. Other accidents happen when people are doing something.

Many people are killed in **natural disasters** each year, too. Natural disasters include storms, fires, and floods.

NEWSFLASH

In the United Kingdom, there are about 199,000 car accidents every year. These kill between 3,200 and 3,500 people.

Violent deaths

Violence also claims many lives. All too often, someone hurts another person so badly that the victim dies. A person might die after a fight or be murdered. He or she might die because of a war or another act of violence. Deaths such as these can be especially hard to **cope** with because they are shocking and should never happen. Some people take their own lives by committing **suicide**.

Accidents, natural disasters, and violence are all shocking because they are unexpected, and because they kill many young people. These events are very painful for everyone involved.

Natural disasters are sudden events that can cause many deaths. Many people were killed in Thailand after the tsunami of 2004.

Different situations

The **circumstances** of a person's death can determine how other people react. All types of death can be difficult for people to cope with. It can be hard for family members and friends to watch a sick person suffer over a long period of time. However, it can also help people to know that they have time to say goodbye to the person.

On the other hand, short illnesses, accidents, and violent deaths can be especially hard on relatives and friends because the death comes as a surprise. In these situations there is little or no time for people to say goodbye. No matter what the cause of death is, every circumstance is unique and painful for the people left behind.

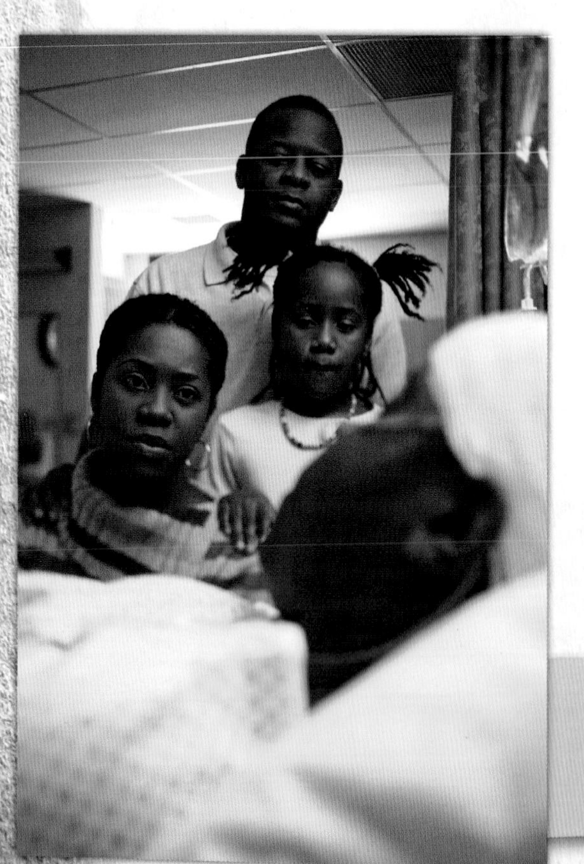

Sometimes people are able to say goodbye to a loved one before he or she dies.

Case study

Matt was a popular teen and the star of his school's rugby team. One afternoon, he left school to drive home for lunch. His car crashed into the side of an overpass, and Matt was killed instantly. Matt's death sent shock waves through his school and the community. His school hired special **counsellors** to help the pupils deal with their grief.

A close relationship will affect how a person feels about a death.

How close were you?

The **relationship** people had with the **deceased** also has an impact on the **survivors' reactions** to the death. The death of a family member who lives with you or a close friend may have a much stronger impact than the death of someone who lives far away or who you do not see very often.

Family matters

For many young people, the death of a grandparent is their first experience with death. This type of death can be very difficult to deal with. However, because most grandparents are older, these deaths may not be as **traumatic**.

The death of a parent can be terrible. Children and teenagers depend on their mothers and fathers for almost everything in their lives, and the loss of such an important person can be tremendously upsetting.

Losing a brother or sister is also very difficult. It is unusual for children and teenagers to die, so this type of death can be shocking. Also, brothers and sisters usually live together. Losing such an important family member can be hard to deal with.

Case study

Karen's grandmother had always lived with Karen's family. Grandma had a bad heart and often felt sick. In time, she got weaker and weaker and had to stay in bed. Karen spent a lot of time with her grandmother. When Grandma died of a heart attack, Karen felt lost.

How do you feel?

Grief is the most common and immediate reaction when someone has died. Grief is the deep and painful sadness people feel when someone they love dies.

Sadness

It is normal to feel sad after someone dies. A person who is grieving misses the family member or friend who has died. People who feel sad often cry or lose interest in activities they used to enjoy. They might want to spend more time alone instead of making the effort to be with other people.

Anger

Many people feel angry when someone they are close to dies. People might feel angry with doctors who could not save that person's life or with people who caused a fatal accident. Sometimes, people even feel angry at the dead person. He or she might blame the person for dying, even though it is not really that person's fault.

It is normal to feel a terrible sadness when someone you love has died.

People find many ways to deal with their feelings after a loved one has died. Music can be a good way to deal with difficult emotions.

Guilt

Someone might feel guilty if he or she had a fight with a person who died not long afterwards. Or the person might feel guilty because he or she could not do anything to save the dead person's life. It is important to remember that no one is perfect, and it is normal to have arguments with people we love.

Loneliness

Loneliness often strikes after someone has died because that person is no longer there. It's normal to miss seeing the person, talking to him or her, and spending time with the person who has died.

Fear

After a close friend or family member dies, people might fear that they or other friends or family members will also die. Survivors might think they will catch the same disease that killed the person, or be in an accident just like the person who has died.

Case study

Mary and Andrew where shocked when they found out that their father was ill with **terminal** cancer. Andrew was angry and got into trouble at school. Mary, on the other hand, was extra helpful to everyone. She told herself that if she acted perfectly, her father would get well. In time, they were both able to accept their father's death and move on with their lives.

Even more emotions

There are other feelings that often occur when a person is faced with death. Many people feel hopeless. They believe that because they can do nothing to change the fact that a loved one has died, they also have no power over other parts of their lives. Someone who feels hopeless often loses interest in activities and life in general.

Some people become confused after a loved one dies. Many people report that they have seen or heard the dead person. Sometimes they "forget" that the person has died and expect to see him or her. These feelings can be scary, but they are normal. It takes a while to get used to the idea that a loved one is really gone.

It is normal to experience many different feelings after a loved one has died.

What do you think?

There are many **euphemisms** for death. For example, someone might say the person is "lost" or has "passed on." Why do you think people use these expressions? Do you think they're helpful or do they just cause confusion and pain?

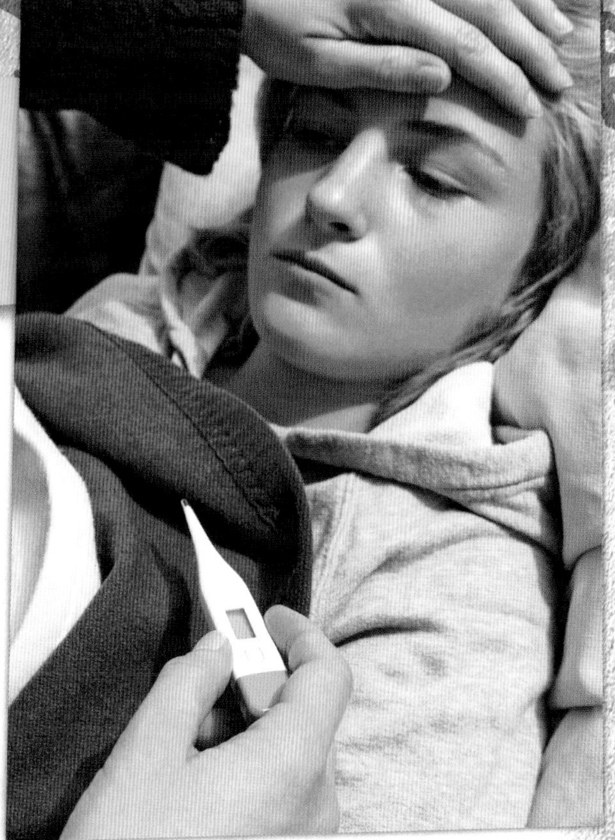

Grief can make a person feel physically ill.

Insensitive people

People don't always understand how it feels to lose a loved one. Even if they do, they may not know how to express their own feelings. It can be especially hard for teenagers to know what to say to a friend because they may not have experienced death before. This means that they want to help but do not know what to say to make someone else feel better.

It can be hard for a person who is grieving to deal with comments from others. If someone says something hurtful or **insensitive**, remember that the person probably has no idea what to say. He or she may feel very uncomfortable talking or thinking about death. The person probably had good **intentions**.

Body and mind

Coping with death and loss can also lead to physical illness. A person can be so upset that he or she actually gets physically sick. Common symptoms from grieving are headaches, stomachaches, and exhaustion. These feelings also come from **stress**. Dealing with the loss of a loved one is one of the most stressful experiences a person can go through.

Top tip

It can be frustrating to deal with insensitive comments while you are grieving. If someone says something that is hurtful, try to remember that the person was probably trying to help. Focus on that instead of the comment that came out of their mouth.

Rituals that help us

Over the years, people have developed many **rituals** to cope with death and comfort other people after someone dies.

Wakes and funerals

Wakes are a very common ritual after someone dies. Wakes are usually held at a **funeral home**. Friends and family come together to **pay respects** and share memories of the person who has died. The dead person is usually at the wake, laid out in a **coffin**. The coffin may be open or closed.

During a **funeral**, people usually read from a religious book, and a religious leader or other representative gives a speech that is meant to comfort those gathered there. Family and friends often participate by doing readings, singing songs, or offering a **eulogy** honouring the dead person. Funerals can get very emotional because they help people recognize and accept that the person has really died, and this may be extremely difficult.

Memorial services are similar to funerals. People gather together to share memories about the deceased person. Memorial services are usually held a few weeks, months, or even years, after the person has died, and the body is not present. Although memorial services are a celebration of the dead person's life, this ritual can be sad because it brings back so many memories of the person who has died.

A funeral is a time for family and friends to comfort each other.

Case study

Sean's mother died suddenly in a plane crash. At the funeral, Sean was surprised to see that all of the benches in the church were filled. There were even people standing in the aisles. Seeing such a crowd made Sean realize that his mother was important to many people, and hearing their stories helped him remember the good times he had shared with his mum.

Sometimes a small memorial is left at the scene of an accident.

New ways to remember

Recently, people have come up with new ways to honour a deceased person's memory. If a person dies in an accident, flowers, candles, soft toys, letters, and photos are often left at the spot of the accident or outside the person's home. These gifts show that other people care about the dead person. They also help people remember the person who has died.

People sometimes create online **tributes** for deceased family members, friends, and relatives. Websites help people share their grief and memories, honour the deceased person for what he or she meant to others, and keep the person's memory alive.

Finding comfort from others

When someone dies, the people who knew him or her reach out to each other in several ways. It is common for people to visit the family, either at the wake or in the days and weeks following the funeral. Many people welcome these visits because it keeps the memory of their loved one alive. Visitors may also try to help the family by bringing food or other gifts, or doing housework and other chores so the family can concentrate on more important things.

Many people send sympathy cards and flowers to the family of someone who has died. Cards and gifts can help the family feel better by letting them know that others are thinking of them and sharing their pain. Cards and flowers can also help the person who sends them. They are a way for the person to express their feelings and provide comfort to the family.

Support from family, friends, and the community can be a great help to people who are grieving.

Helping others

Today it is common for a family to request **donations** to a charity in memory of their deceased loved one. The charity may be a hospital or **hospice** that helped the family during an illness, or it may be an organization that the deceased person belonged to or strongly believed in. Many people see charitable donations as a way to make a difference and bring some good out of a sad loss.

Many people send sympathy cards to the family of a dead person. These cards show they are thinking of the family and remembering the person who has died.

Case study

Angela was born with a serious heart defect and died when she was 12 years old. Many people in the community donated money to the hospital where Angela had been treated. A year after her death, the community even held a 5 km race that raised money for the hospital. The tremendous amount of support comforted Angela's family and helped them to realize that other people had also loved Angela.

Coping with death

Everyone has their own way of grieving. There is no "right" or "wrong" way to express emotions and get used to the fact that a loved one has died.

Alone or together

Some people may want to be alone with their feelings. They may withdraw from family and friends. They might spend time in their room or in activities by themselves. They will no longer hang out with friends or take part in sports, clubs, or other activities.

Others may seek out other people so they don't feel so lonely and scared. It may look like these survivors don't care about the death or have forgotten that the person died. However, they are just finding a way of coping with the death that works for them.

Similarly, one family member might want to talk about the deceased all the time, because he or she finds it comforting to think about the dead person. Another family member may get upset whenever the dead person is mentioned because he or she finds it sad to be reminded of the person who died. It is important for families to try to help each other through difficult times.

Some people visit a cemetery where a loved one is buried to feel close to the person who has died.

Get over it?

There is also no set time to "get over" a death. Some people may seem like their old selves within a few weeks or months, while others might grieve for years. A person might also present a happy face to the world and act like everything is okay, but still feel sad and angry and cry at home, where no one can see.

All these reactions are normal. A person will move on and accept the situation when he or she is ready. This can take a short amount of time, or it may take forever. No one can change that timing.

Case study

One day, Cath and her brother, Sam, went for a walk. A few streets from home, they were hit by a car. Cath was hurt, but Sam died. Cath missed her brother very much. The house seemed empty without him. It also hurt to go to school and see his friends and know Sam was not there any more.

Taking part in a community event in memory of a loved one can be a good way to honour someone who has died.

It can take a long time for some people to return to normal activities after the death of a loved one.

Daily routines

Returning to school after the death of a loved one can be very tough. Other pupils may not know what to say to a person who is grieving. You may feel alone, and may not want things to get back to normal. However, returning to your usual activities can help you maintain a normal life.

Activities

It is important to take part in your usual activities. Your life should not stop because a loved one has died. It's normal to want to take a break or stay away from everyone for a while, but in time, it's good to get back into a familiar **routine**.

It's also a good idea to try new activities. Finding a new hobby or fun way to spend time can make you feel energized and excited again. It can also help you make new friends and start a new routine that may help you let go of some of the sadness.

It can be hard to celebrate happy occasions when a person who has died is not there to share the good times with you.

Holidays, birthdays, and other special times

It can be awkward and sad to celebrate special times after someone has died. Many people find it hard to feel happy when a loved one is gone. People who usually look forward to holidays and birthdays with eagerness may now have difficulty facing these days.

Many families do not celebrate holidays for months or even years after someone has died. Other families try to keep things exactly the same. In time, family members and friends may find new **traditions**. They may celebrate special times in a new way, while honouring the deceased person during the celebration.

It is important to remember that moving forwards with your life does not mean that you are forgetting your loved one. The person who died would not want you to be unhappy and would want you to enjoy your life.

Top tips

Here are some ways to remember a loved one:

- Be creative. Draw a picture, write a song, or write a poem that expresses how you feel.
- Make a memory book, a scrapbook, or a photo collage that shows moments you shared with the person who died.
- Plant a tree or other plant to remember the deceased person.
- Talk to other people who are grieving the loss of the deceased person. Share your memories.
- Do something to honour the person, such as donating to a charity or taking part in an activity the person enjoyed.

Reaching out

Dealing with death is very difficult, and many people cannot do it alone. Sometimes people need extra help to grieve and accept their loss. There are many sources of help.

Family

The family can be the most powerful source of support after a person experiences the death of a loved one. Talking to parents, siblings, and other family members can be a big help. These people probably knew the loved one too and may share your feelings. Also, adults have probably had to cope with death before and will have the experience to understand your feelings and help you grieve and understand what happened.

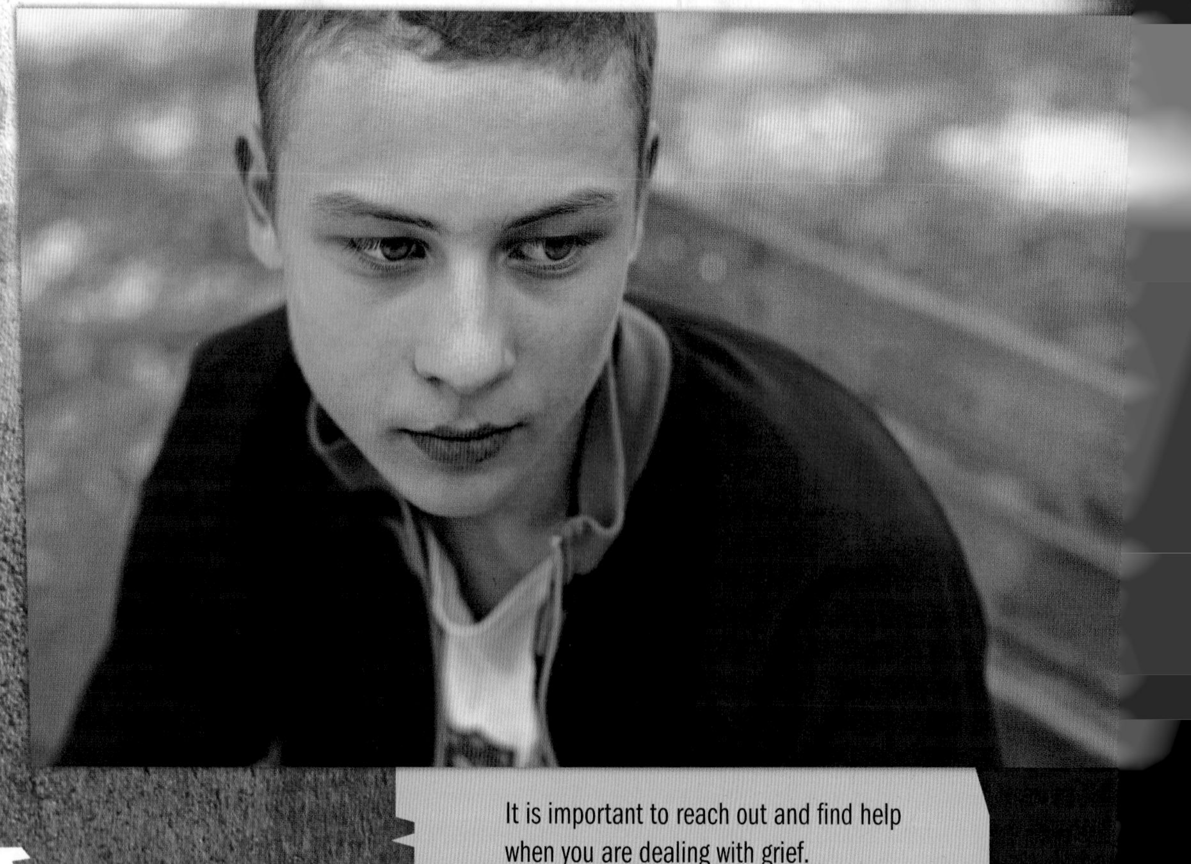

It is important to reach out and find help when you are dealing with grief.

How about friends?

Friends can also be a good source of support. While some friends may feel awkward about the death because they are scared and upset themselves, most will want to help. Find a friend or two you really trust and let them know you need their help. Often, just finding someone who will listen to you can make you feel better.

However, there are many teenagers who have not experienced death first-hand. A person who has not had a loved one die may not be able to understand or help you with your feelings. For this reason, a friend who has previously experienced a loss could be a good person to share with.

A trusted adult can be the best source of support for teenagers dealing with someone's death.

Case study

Robbie felt lost when his father died after a short struggle with cancer. His father had been very involved in Robbie's life, and Robbie could not imagine how he could go on without him. Then his friend Darren told him that he was lucky to have had such a special father-son relationship. Robbie realized that his friend was right and began to feel that life still held good things for him.

More sources of help

If you need more help than friends and family members can give you, you might want to talk to a counsellor or a **therapist**. A school counsellor is a good place to start. These people are trained to deal with grief and may be able to help you work through your feelings.

Many people seek help from a religious counsellor. A minister, priest, rabbi, or other religious official also receives training to deal with grief and loss and may be able to help you find meaning in a loved one's death.

A school counsellor can be one source of support for grieving young people.

What do you think?

Some organizations hold picnics or fairs where grieving children and teenagers get together to talk about their experiences with others who have gone through the same thing. Some people welcome the chance to share their feelings, while others might feel it is too hard to do this. Do you think attending one of these events is a helpful way to cope?

Changing lives

Life is full of changes. Death can bring big changes to a person's life. If a parent dies, the surviving parent might get married again. Friends may drift away and new friends may come along who will make survivors see life in a new way. Some people resist these changes. They may feel that getting used to a new life means that they don't care about the dead person anymore. This is not true.

Moving on

Just as it is normal to grieve in your own way, it is also okay to move on with your life while still remembering the past. This does not mean that you have forgotten the person you loved. When someone is coping with the death of a loved one, he or she may feel like things will never be good again. However, most people do learn to remember the person they lost and are still able to enjoy life. If you are grieving the death of a loved one, believe that you will feel better with time. You will feel happy and "normal" again.

People often find that expressing themselves through art helps them feel better and cope with things happening in their lives. It is important for you to find a way to cope that works for you.

Facts about death

- Young people understand death differently at different ages. Children under five years old do not understand that death is forever. They may expect the dead person to come back, even after they have been told about death and maybe even went to the funeral. Older children and teenagers understand that death is the end of life and the person will not be back again.

- Most African countries have a life expectancy of less than 65 years. One reason is because people in this part of the world do not have access to medicine, clean water, and plenty of food. In North America, Europe, and Australia, life expectancies are more than 76 years.

- Today, players on sports teams often wear a black armband on one sleeve of their uniform to honour a player or coach who has died.

- One hundred years ago, most people died at home. Today, most people die in hospitals, and funeral directors prepare the body. Many people feel that removing death from our everyday lives makes it harder to understand that death is a natural part of life.

- The colour black is a symbol of death in Western countries, such as the UK and countries in Europe. In Eastern countries, such as China, white is a symbol of death.

- Hospice care is appealing to many families of people with a terminal illness. Hospices provide end-of-life care that focuses on managing pain and allowing people to die in comfortable surroundings while being with their loved ones. Hospice care can be given at home, in a hospice centre, or in a nursing home or other facility.

Glossary

circumstance facts or conditions connected to an event

coffin container in which a dead person is placed for burial

cope deal with

counsellor someone who is trained to help people with their problems

deceased dead person

disease illness

donation money or items given to a person or organization to help them

eulogy speech that honours or praises someone who has died

euphemism pleasant expression that substitutes for another phrase

fatal something that causes death

funeral ceremony held after someone has died

funeral home place where bodies are prepared for viewing and burial

grief extreme sadness

hospice organization or place that cares for people who are terminally ill

insensitive thoughtless

intention thing a person means to do

memorial service gathering where people share memories of someone who has died

natural causes death from old age or disease

natural disaster severe weather or other dangerous occurrence in nature

pay respects to visit a family and express sympathy at the loss of a loved one

reaction action in response to something

relationship way in which people get on with each other

ritual set of actions that is performed as part of a ceremony

routine usual habits and way of life

stress worry, strain, or pressure

suicide when a person takes his or her own life

survivor person who lives after other people have died

terminal something that cannot be cured

therapist person who is trained to deal with emotional problems

tradition belief and custom followed by a group of people

traumatic extremely upsetting or shocking

tribute something that honours or remembers a dead person

violence using physical force to injure or abuse someone or something

wake gathering where people view a dead person's body and comfort his or her family and friends

Further resources

Death is difficult to cope with. If you are dealing with the death of a loved one, remember that you aren't alone. As well as your family and friends, there are many resources available to help you cope with death.

Books

Choices and Decisions: When People Die, Pete Sanders and Steve Myers (Franklin Watts, 2005)

Death, Janine Amos (Cherrytree Books, 2007)

Websites

Child bereavement
www.childbereavement.org.uk/for_young_people
This website has advice for young people on lots of issues surrounding the death of someone close.

Childline
www.childline.org.uk/ContactChildLine.asp
Contact details for Childline are on this page. They can help with whatever problems you may have.

Coping with grief
www.bbc.co.uk/relationships/coping_with_grief/bereavement_effectschildren.shtml
This web page covers the reactions of children of all ages to the death of someone close to them. It can help to show that you're not alone in having to deal with death at a young age.

Websites (continued)

Noah's Ark Trust
www.communigate.co.uk/worcs/noahsarktrust/index.phtml
Noah's Ark Trust was set up in Worcestershire to offer help and support to bereaved young people in the area.

RD4U
www.rd4u.org.uk/personal/index.html
This site gives advice on how to deal with the death of a loved one and tries to show that it's okay to express your feelings.

Winston's wish
www.winstonswish.org.uk/foryoungpeople/ask/
Click on "A–Z" to see brief explanations for a number of different parts of the grieving process.

Organization

The Compassionate Friends
53 North Street
Bristol BS3 1EN
Tel helpline: 0845 123 2304
Website: www.compassionatefriends.org.uk
The Compassionate Friends works to assist families who have lost a child of any age.

Index